Electric Gadgets and Gizmos

Battery-powered buildable gadgets that go!

Written by
Alan Bartholomew

Illustrated by
Lynn Bartholomew

Kids Can Press

**This book is dedicated to our kids, Chrissy and Al Jr.,
and to all those who are committed to the care and nurturing of children,
especially our parents. – A.B. and L.B.**

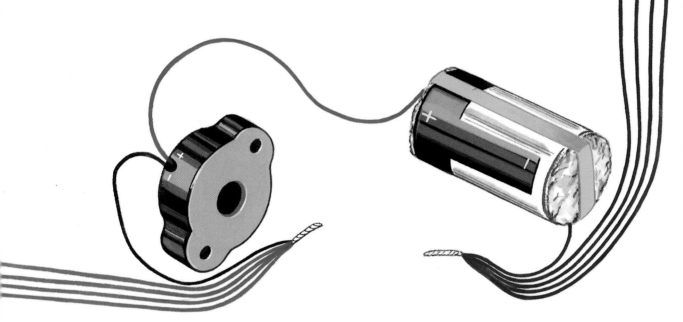

Text copyright © 1998 by Alan Bartholomew
Illustrations copyright © 1998 by Lynn Bartholomew

KIDS CAN DO IT and the ▇ logo are trade marks of
Kids Can Press Ltd.

Published in Canada by
Kids Can Press Ltd.
29 Birch Avenue
Toronto, ON M4V 1E2

Published in the U.S. by
Kids Can Press Ltd.
85 River Rock Drive, Suite 202
Buffalo, NY 14207

Edited by Laurie Wark and Trudee Romanek
Designed by Marie Bartholomew
Printed in Hong Kong by Wing King Tong Co. Ltd.

CM 98 0 9 8 7 6 5 4

Canadian Cataloguing in Publication Data

Bartholomew, Alan

Electric gadgets and gizmos : battery-powered
buildable gadgets that go!

(Kids can do it)
ISBN 1-55074-439-9

1. Electric apparatus and appliances – Juvenile literature.
2. Electricity – Experiments – Juvenile literature.
I. Bartholomew, Lynn. II. Title. III. Series.

TK148.B37 1998   j621.31'042   C97–931621–9

Kids Can Press is a Nelvana company

Contents

Introduction

Would you like to make your own electric gadgets? For more than ten years now, I have been building projects with kids of all ages. Together we've improved our designs and come up with the gizmos you'll find here, like the wacky windshield-wiper glasses or the surprising gift box that rumbles when someone picks it up.

Try to do the projects in this book in order, since they progress from the simplest to the most challenging. And if you see a symbol like this one (👫), it means that step is harder or could be dangerous. Ask an adult for some help.

The first pages will tell you about the materials you need to collect. You can find most of them around your home or at hardware stores. Then read on to discover how to make battery connections and switches and you'll be ready to start your first project.
Happy wiring!

In all the projects, you'll be making a basic circle circuit like this one. Always check all the connections in the circuit. If any part of the circle is broken, the electric gadget won't work.

Materials

Batteries

Every project in this book requires either a 1.5 or 6.0 volt (V) battery. Any brand should do, but Energizer batteries were used to test these gadgets.

The size of a battery is also important; not all 1.5 V batteries will fit in all gadgets. The projects in this book require 1.5 V batteries in only C or D cell sizes.

A battery is a source of direct current (DC), which means the electricity in it flows in only one direction. The positive (+) and negative (-) signs on the battery show which way the electricity will flow.

Modern battery brands do not contain toxic materials such as mercury or cadmium. Old or "dead" batteries can be disposed of in normal household garbage or, in some communities, taken to a special drop-off point.

Safety note

Each project uses a low-voltage battery source. **Never use electricity from a household wall outlet** because the amount of electricity is very dangerous.

C cell battery (1.5 v)

D cell battery (1.5 v)

6 volt battery

Continued on next page ⟶

Buzzers

You can use any type of electric bell or buzzer that makes a sound and works with a small battery, 6.0 V or less. Available in hardware or hobby stores.

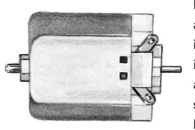

2.5 volt motor

2.5 volt buzzer

Motors

Motors used in the projects are the same as those found in most toys. They are small in size, from 1.5 to 3.0 V DC, and come in many different shapes. Available from hobby or science stores.

2.5 volt motor

3.0 volt motor

1.5 volt motor

Bulbs

The same as those found in most handheld flashlights, usually 1.5 to 3.0 V, any shape or color. They are available in hardware or hobby stores.

1.5 volt bulb

2.5 volt bulb

double strand

single strand

Wire

Wire is measured by thickness, or gauge. These projects require 14 or 24 gauge wire, either single- or double-strand. ("Single strand" means one insulated wire. "Double strand" means two, attached.) If you can't find 24 gauge single-strand wire, buy quad hook-up wire that is used to connect telephones. Remove its plastic insulation with a utility knife or scissors and use the four individual insulated wires inside. For projects that require 24 gauge double-strand wire, use doorbell or speaker wire.

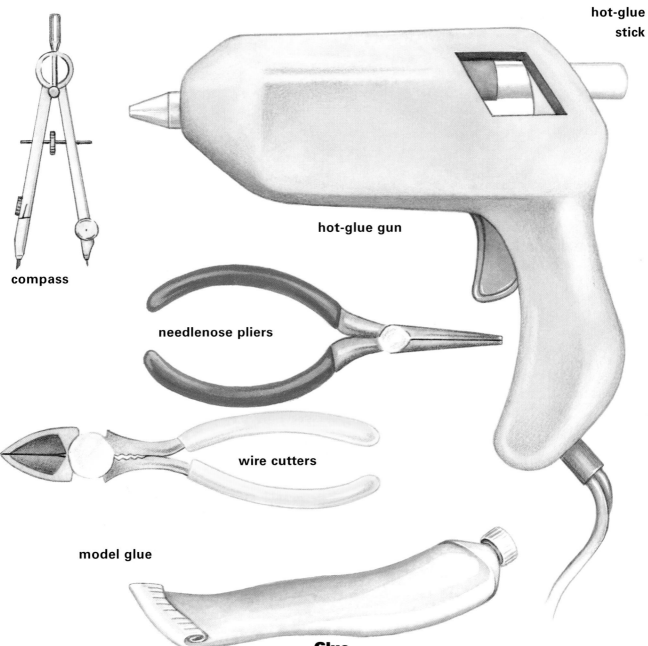

hot-glue stick

hot-glue gun

compass

needlenose pliers

wire cutters

model glue

screws

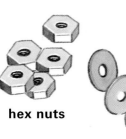

hex nuts

washers

Glue

Any kind of glue may be used, such as white craft glue, model glue or fast-drying glue. A low-temperature hot-glue gun is recommended because the glue dries quickly and securely. Ask an adult for permission to use a hot-glue gun, and be careful not to get glue on your skin. Each time you finish using a glue gun, put it down safely in a clear spot on your work table. Remember to unplug it when you're done.

Making Battery Connections

The projects in this book require battery connections for power. Each project specifies what kind of batteries you need and whether you require a battery pad or pack. Refer to these pages for instructions on how to construct them.

Battery pad

1 Trace around your battery on a piece of cardboard and cut out the circle.

2 To find the center of the circle, fold it in half twice. Use a sharp pencil or scissors to punch a small hole in the center.

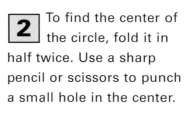

3 Use open scissors to remove 8 cm (3 in.) of plastic insulation from one end of the wire.

4 Poke the bare wire through the hole in the cardboard circle and wrap it around the circle.

5 Wrap the circle in aluminum foil, leaving the covered end of wire sticking out. This is the contact pad that will connect the battery to the project circuit.

You will need

a pencil and scissors
a battery
(as specified in each project)

cardboard (from a cereal box)

20 cm (8 in.) of wire
(24 gauge, single strand)

aluminum foil

Battery pack

1 Trace your battery on the pie plate twice and cut out the two circles.

2 Use the nail to punch two holes in the side of the bottle, one at the top and one at the bottom.

You will need

a pencil and scissors

a C cell battery (1.5 V)

an aluminum foil pie plate

a small nail

a black plastic film container or round pill bottle (large enough to hold a C cell battery) and lid

2 pieces of wire, each 20 cm (8 in.) long (24 gauge, single strand)

3 Use open scissors to remove 8 cm (3 in.) of insulation from one end of each wire.

4 Wind the bare end of one wire into a coil about the size of a dime.

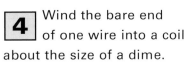

5 Feed the covered end of this wire into the bottle and out the bottom hole so that the coil is in the bottom of the bottle.

6 Push one of the aluminum circles into the bottle so that it touches the wire.

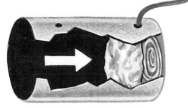

7 Drop the battery into the bottle so that its negative end is touching the aluminum circle.

8 Curl the bare end of the other wire so that it fits into the lid, and cover it with the other aluminum circle.

9 Thread the other end of the wire in through the top of the bottle and out the top hole.

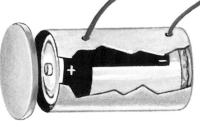

10 Put the lid on the bottle, closing it tightly. As the lid is pushed down, it will squeeze the wires and aluminum circles into contact with the positive and negative ends of the battery, making a good connection.

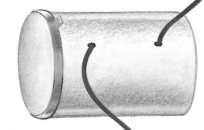

Making Switches

All the projects in this book require a switch to turn them on and off. These are two of the most common types. Refer to these pages when you're making a switch for your gadget.

Push-button switch

1 Using scissors, remove 8 cm (3 in.) of insulation from the end of each wire coming from your gadget.

2 Wrap the bare end of one piece of wire tightly around one of the legs of the clothespin. Do the same with the second wire on the other leg of the clothespin.

3 As you push on the clothespin to open it, the legs and wires are squeezed together, causing the switch to close. (A closed switch means the gadget is on.)

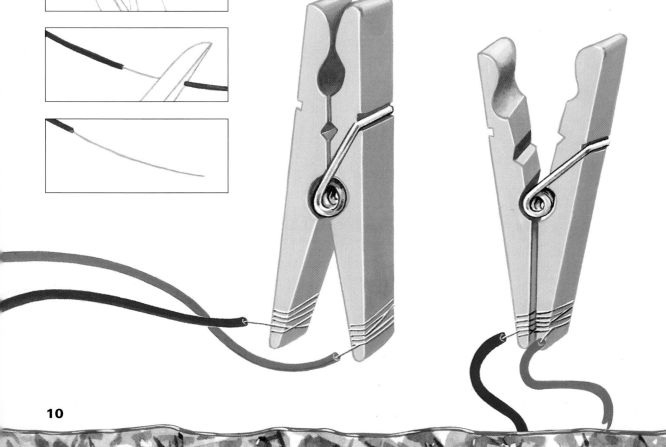

Hook switch

1 Using scissors, remove 5 cm (2 in.) of insulation from one end of one wire and 9 cm (3½ in.) from one end of the other wire.

2 Wrap a piece of tape around the Popsicle stick 0.5 cm (¼ in.) from each end.

3 Press a pin through each piece of tape into the Popsicle stick, leaving 0.5 cm (¼ in.) of the pin showing above the stick.

4 Wrap the bare 5 cm (2 in.) piece of wire tightly around one pin.

5 Wrap the bare 9 cm (3½ in.) piece of wire around the other pin, this time leaving 8 cm (3 in.) of bare wire sticking out.

6 To close the switch, hook this bare wire around the first pin. Removing this wire hook will open the switch and turn the gadget off.

You will need

scissors

2 pieces of wire, each 20 cm (8 in.) long (24 gauge, single-strand)

masking tape

a Popsicle stick

push pins or tacks

Flashlight

1 Trace a circle slightly bigger than the tube on the cardboard, cut it out, and make a large hole in the center with a sharp pencil or scissors.

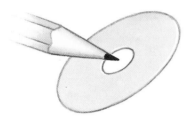

2 Cut a piece of wire 20 cm (8 in.) long and remove 5 cm (2 in.) of insulation from each end.

You will need

a battery pad (see page 8)

a pencil and scissors

cardboard (from a cereal box)

wire (24 gauge, single strand)

a lightbulb (1.5 V)

a toilet-tissue tube

masking tape

a D cell battery (1.5 V)

tissues

a clothespin

glue

3 Wrap one of the bare ends around the base of the bulb and push the base through the hole in the cardboard circle. Secure it with a drop of glue. This is the light pad.

4 Cut the tube to the same length as the clothespin. Use a pencil or scissors to punch a hole in the side of the tube.

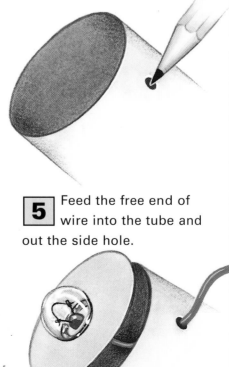

5 Feed the free end of wire into the tube and out the side hole.

6 Push the battery-pad wire into the other end of the tube and out the same hole. Push the pad into the end of the tube and tape over the end so the battery pad won't fall out.

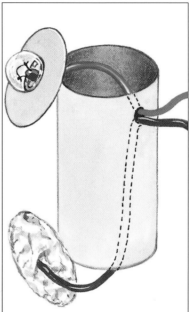

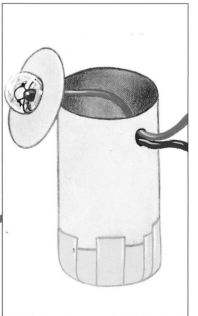

7 Slide the battery into the tube positive end down. Pack around it with tissues so it doesn't move. Push the light pad into the tube so that the base of the lightbulb touches the battery's negative end. Tape the light pad in place.

8 Connect the wires to make a push-button switch. Wrap the bare end of wire from the light pad around one of the legs of the clothespin. Remove 5 cm (2 in.) of insulation from the battery-pad wire. Wrap it around the other leg. (See page 10.)

9 Test your flashlight by pushing the two clothespin legs together until the wires touch and the lightbulb comes on. If it doesn't work, check that the wires are connected, or try pressing the lightbulb onto the battery to make a better contact.

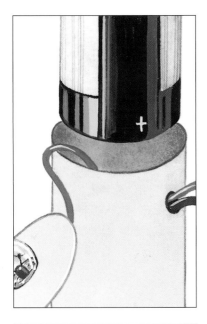

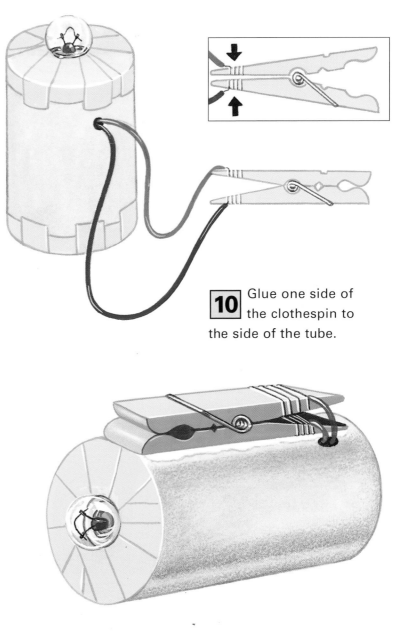

10 Glue one side of the clothespin to the side of the tube.

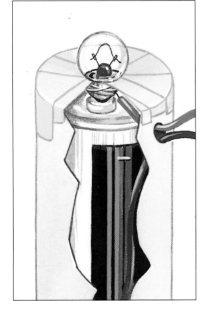

Hand Fan

1 Use a pencil or scissors to punch a small hole in the side of the cardboard tube. Push the wire from one battery pad into the tube and out the hole. Tape over the end so the battery pad won't fall out.

4 Slide the battery into the tube positive end down. Pack around it with tissues so it doesn't move. Push the other battery pad inside the tube, leaving the loose wire poking out from the top.

2 Cut a piece of wire 20 cm (8 in.) long and remove 2.5 cm (1 in.) of insulation from one end.

3 Wrap the bare end of this wire around one of the two connector tabs on the motor. Secure it with a drop of glue. Poke the other end into the top of the tube and out the hole in the side.

5 Remove 5 cm (2 in.) of insulation from this loose wire. Wrap the bare wire around the motor's other connector tab. Secure it with a drop of glue.

You will need

2 battery pads (see page 8)

a pencil and scissors

a toilet-tissue tube

masking tape

wire (24 gauge, single strand)

a small DC motor (1.5 V)

a D cell battery (1.5 V)

tissues

a clothespin

glue

a utility knife

a bottle cork

a Popsicle stick (or a propeller, available at craft and hobby stores)

6 Remove 5 cm (2 in.) of insulation from the two remaining wires.

7 Connect these wires to make a push-button switch (see page 10). Test your connection by pushing the clothespin legs together until the wires touch and your fan motor comes on. If it doesn't work, check the wire connections or the battery contact. Glue the switch onto the tube.

8 Tuck in the motor wires. Glue the motor to the inside of the tube so that its shaft, the part that spins, is pointing out.

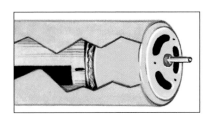

9 Cut a 1 cm (¹/₂ in.) slice from the cork and press it onto the motor shaft.

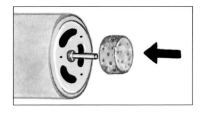

10 Glue the Popsicle stick onto the cork to act as the fan blade. As the motor spins, it will turn the cork, causing the Popsicle-stick blade to turn, too.

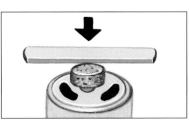

Communication Buzzer

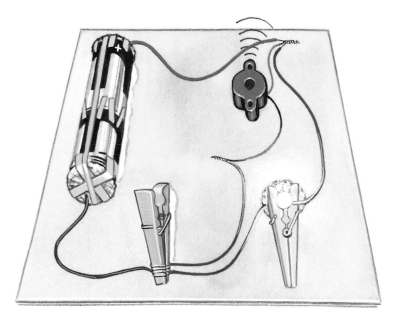

1 Remove 10 cm (4 in.) of insulation from the wire of a battery pad and wrap it around one of the legs of a clothespin.

2 Tape this pad to the negative end of one battery.

3 Remove 10 cm (4 in.) of insulation from the wire of a second battery pad and wrap it around the other leg of the same clothespin.

4 Glue the clothespin and the second battery pad onto the cardboard about 5 cm (2 in.) apart.

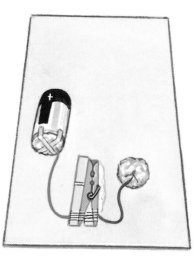

5 Place the second clothespin on top of the battery pad on the cardboard. Position this clothespin so that the hole in the closed end is on top of the pad.

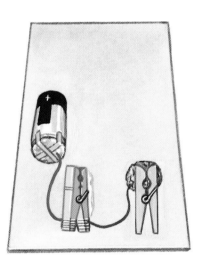

6 Cut two 20 cm (8 in.) pieces of wire. Remove 10 cm (4 in.) of insulation from one end and 2.5 cm (1 in.) from the other end of both pieces.

7 Wrap the 10 cm (4 in.) bare end of one wire around the base of the lightbulb. Open the clothespin that is placed on top of the second battery pad and slide the base of the bulb into the hole in the clamping end. Push down on the lightbulb so that it touches the aluminum foil of the pad and glue the clothespin in place.

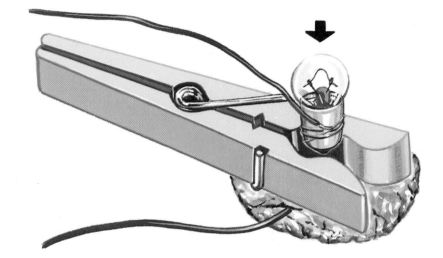

8 Remove 2.5 cm (1 in.) of insulation from the wire of the third battery pad and from the buzzer's red wire. Twist these two bare ends together with the bare end of the lightbulb wire.

9 Tape this battery pad to the positive end of the second battery, then tape the two batteries together so that the positive end of one touches the negative end of the other. Stretch the elastic over the length of the two batteries to help keep them in contact with each other. Glue them to the cardboard base.

10 Wrap the 10 cm (4 in.) bare end of remaining wire (from step 6) around the same leg of the clothespin as in step 3. Strip 2.5 cm (1 in.) of insulation from the black buzzer wire and twist it together with the other end of this wire. Test your light and buzzer.

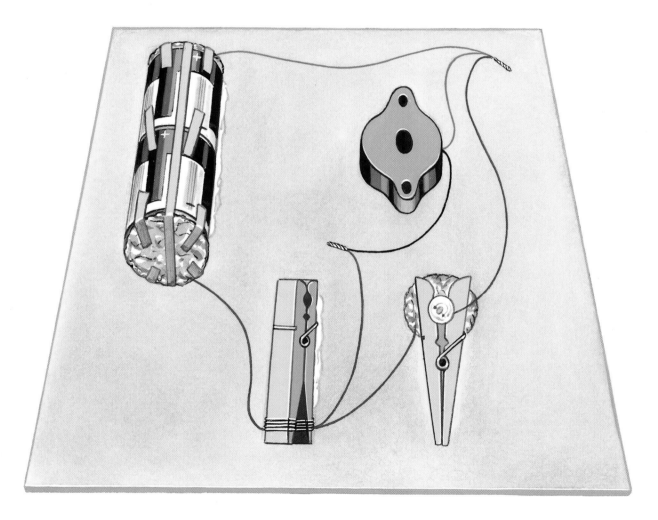

11 Using the examples, make up a code and copy it onto the cardboard. Send a coded message to a friend by pressing on the clothespin — a short time for a dot (•), longer for a dash (–). If you know Morse code, use that.

•	••	•••	—•	—••	—•••	——•	——••	———•••	———••••
you	me	us	come	go	stay	room	yard	house	school

Other Ideas

● Turn your buzzer into a doorbell. Connect a long piece of double-strand wire to the switch and add a second push-button switch at the end of the wire, in another room.

● Make a second buzzer for a friend so you can send messages back and forth. If you want to communicate over a long distance, you'll need two pieces of very long double-strand wire and you'll have to mount your buzzer on your friend's cardboard and his buzzer on yours. If your buzzer doesn't sound, untwist the black connection and the red connection and switch them.

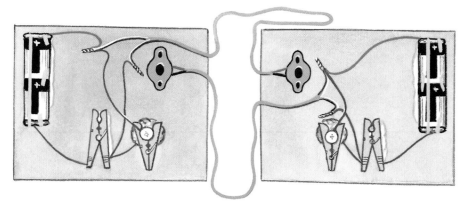

● To operate your communicator in silent mode, disconnect the red buzzer wire and use only the lightbulb.

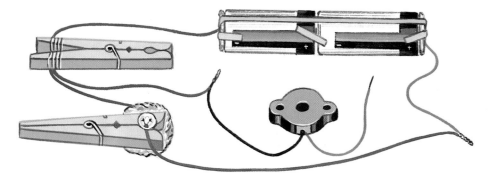

Remote Boat

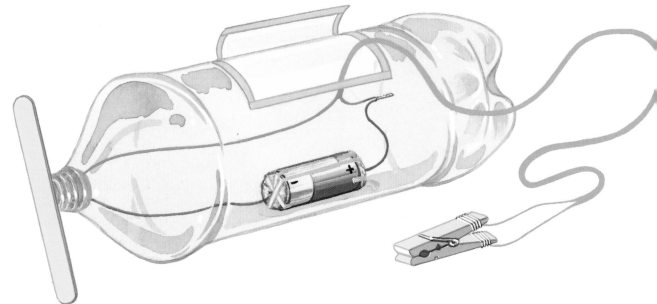

You will need

2 battery pads (see page 8)

masking tape

a D cell battery (1.5 V)

a small elastic band

a DC motor (1.5 V)
(no wider than 22 mm [$^7/_8$ in.])

glue

scissors

wire
(24 gauge, double strand)

an empty 2 L (8 c.)
plastic drink bottle

a utility knife

a bottle cork

a Popsicle stick

a clothespin

1 Tape a battery pad to each end of the battery and stretch the elastic around both ends to hold the pads tightly against the battery.

2 Remove 2.5 cm (1 in.) of insulation from both battery-pad wires. Tightly connect one wire to one of the motor's connector tabs. Add a drop of glue.

3 Cut a piece of double-strand wire 1.5 m (5 ft.) long. Remove 2.5 cm (1 in.) of insulation from all four ends.

4 Connect one of the bare ends of one strand of wire to the motor's other connector tab. Add a drop of glue.

5 Connect the bare end of the other strand of wire to the bare wire of the second battery pad. Test your connections by touching the two remaining bare ends of double-strand wire together. The motor should come on.

6 Cut a hole in the side of the bottle big enough for the battery and motor to fit through. Cover the rough edges with tape. Place the battery and motor inside the bottle. Glue the battery in place.

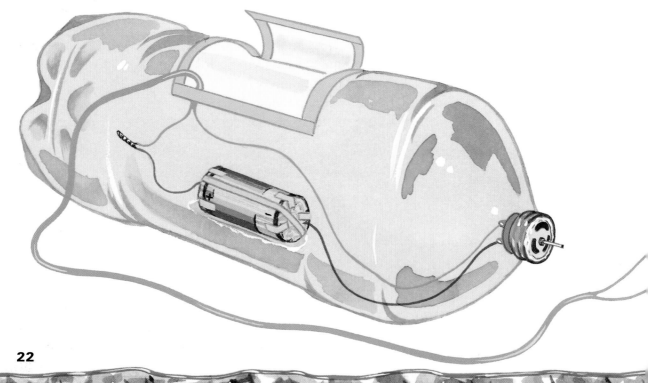

7 Slide the motor inside the neck of the bottle so that its shaft, or narrow end, is pointing out. Put some glue around the outside of the motor to hold it in place and to prevent water from getting in. Don't get glue on the motor's shaft or it will not turn. Tape the hole shut or leave it open as a cargo hold.

8 Cut a slice of cork 1 cm ($^3/_8$ in.) thick and push it onto the shaft of the motor.

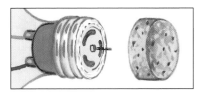

9 Glue the Popsicle stick onto the cork. Let the glue dry. The stick will act as the propeller. As the motor turns the cork, it will also turn the stick, making the boat go. If the boat bounces, trim the Popsicle stick.

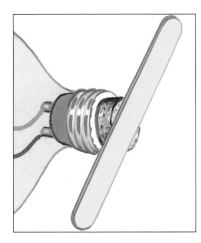

10 Finish your gadget by making a push-button switch with the remaining bare ends of wire (see page 10).

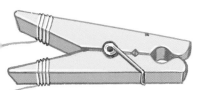

Other Ideas

- Add a lightbulb or buzzer to your boat.

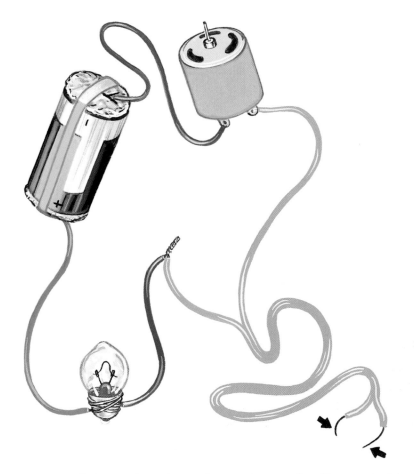

- Leave off the cork and attach a real propeller (from a hobby store) to give the boat more power.

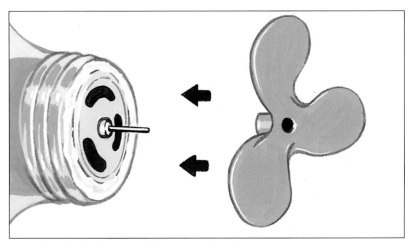

Squirt Finger

You will need

a marker and scissors

2 round plastic bottles
(empty 1 L [4 c.] shampoo
bottles work well)

glue

a small water pump
(available at hardware stores)

plastic tubing, 60 cm x 0.5 cm
(24 in. x $\frac{1}{4}$ in.)

a pin or needle

wire
(24 gauge, double strand)

masking tape

aluminum foil

2 clothespins

a battery (6 V)

a belt

1 Use scissors to make a hole as wide as the open end of the pump in the bottom of one plastic bottle. Glue the pump into the hole.

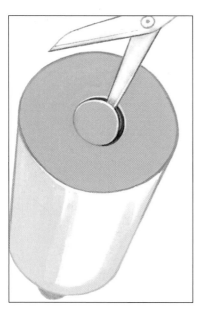

2 Slide the tubing onto the small output hole on the pump and glue around the edges to make sure it doesn't leak.

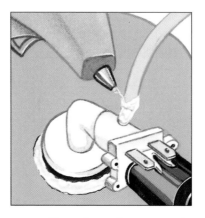

3 Plug the other end of tubing with glue. When the glue is dry, make a small hole in it with a pin.

4 Cut a piece of double-strand wire 60 cm (24 in.) long and remove 10 cm (4 in.) of insulation from one end of both strands and 2.5 cm (1 in.) from the other end of both strands.

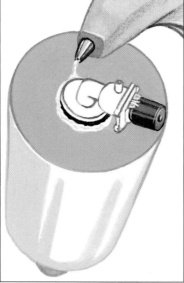

5 Wrap one of the 10 cm (4 in.) bare ends of wire around the plugged end of tubing about 2.5 cm (1 in.) from the end. Put a small piece of aluminum foil over it, and tape around each end of the foil. Make sure the middle section is uncovered. This is one part of the finger switch.

6 Cut another piece of double-strand wire 30 cm (12 in.) long and remove 10 cm (4 in.) of insulation from one end of both strands and 2.5 cm (1 in.) from the other end of both strands.

8 Cut 10 cm (4 in.) from the bottom of the second bottle, and put the battery inside.

7 Wrap one 10 cm (4 in.) piece of bare wire around one side of the clamping end of a clothespin. Cover it with aluminum foil. Repeat this step using the second 10 cm (4 in.) piece of bare wire and a second clothespin.

9 Cut two 2.5 cm (1 in.) slits about 6 cm (2 in.) apart in the side of this bottle. Slide the belt through the slits so that the container hangs from it. You may have to adjust the size of the slits depending on the width of the belt.

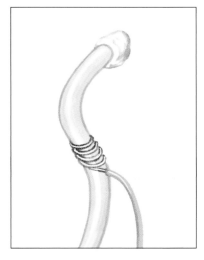

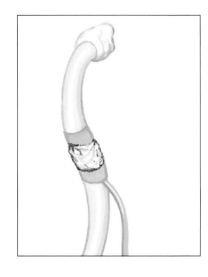

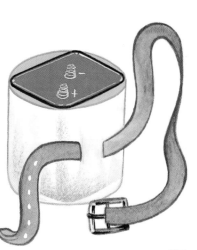

10 Cut two more slits, about the same size as the width of your belt, near the top of the pump bottle. Mark the bottle just below the slits so you'll know where to stop filling the bottle with water.

12 With the wire on the inside, tape the foil into a ring that fits around your finger. This is the other part of the finger switch from step 5. When the gadget is complete, touching these two foil parts together will act as a switch, closing the circuit and turning on the pump.

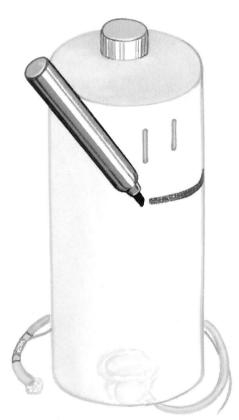

11 Fold a piece of foil into a strip about 2 cm x 8 cm ($^3/_4$ in. x 3 in.). Tape the remaining 10 cm (4 in.) bare strand of wire onto this strip lengthwise.

13 Connect the rest of the wires as shown. Fill the pump bottle with water and screw on the cap. Put the pump bottle on the belt and strap the belt around your waist.

14 Clamp the clothespins from step 7 onto the battery contacts. Test your gadget by touching the foil on the finger ring to the foil contact on the tube. The pump should come on and the water should start squirting out a few seconds later. If the pump works but the water doesn't come out, try switching the clothespins on the battery.

Other Ideas

• Add a second 6 V battery in series (see diagram) to increase the pump's voltage. This will make the pump work faster and give it some extra strength, for those really long shots.

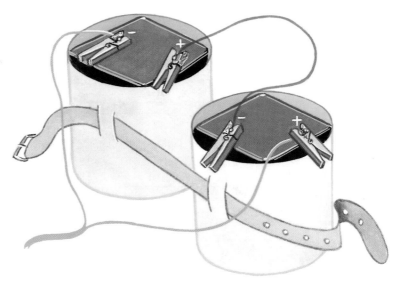

• Add a buzzer or a lightbulb for special effects.

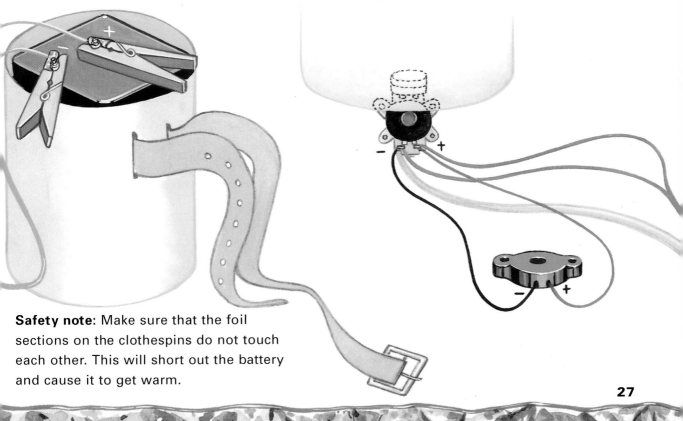

Safety note: Make sure that the foil sections on the clothespins do not touch each other. This will short out the battery and cause it to get warm.

Warning Sign

You will need

2 battery pads (see page 8)

2 D cell batteries (1.5 V)

masking tape

a small elastic band

glue

an empty cereal box

construction paper
(same size as front of box)

utility knife

a pencil and scissors

3 sheets of aluminum foil
(same size as front of box)

wire
(24 gauge, single strand)

2 small lightbulbs (1.5 V)

wire
(24 gauge, double-strand)

2 pieces of cardboard, each
25 cm (10 in.) square

an old sock or thick piece of
fabric

1 Tape the batteries together with the positive end of one pressed against the negative end of the other.

2 Tape a battery pad to each end of the battery stack, and stretch an elastic over the length of the batteries to keep them in contact with the pads.

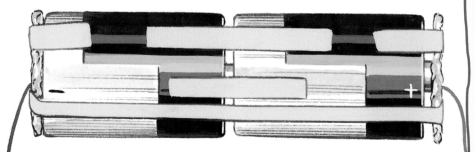

3 Glue the construction paper to the cereal box and cut out the words "KEEP OUT" or a warning symbol.

4 Turn the box over and trace a border 2.5 cm (1 in.) from the edge.

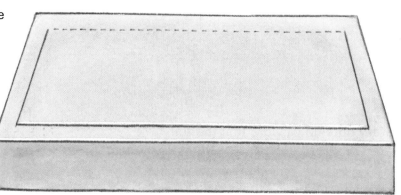

5 Cut out three sides of the border, making a door into the back of the box.

6 Tape one piece of aluminum foil to the inside of the door, shiny side out. Use a sharp pencil to punch two small holes in the middle of the door. Each hole should be big enough to hold one lightbulb.

7 Cut two pieces of single-strand wire 20 cm (8 in.) long. Remove 8 cm (3 in.) of insulation from one end of each piece and 2.5 cm (1 in.) from the other end of each piece. Wrap one 8 cm (3 in.) bare end of wire around the base of each lightbulb.

8 Push each lightbulb into a hole in the box door, keeping the bulbs and wire inside the box. Glue the base of each bulb securely to the cardboard. Twist the bare ends of wire together.

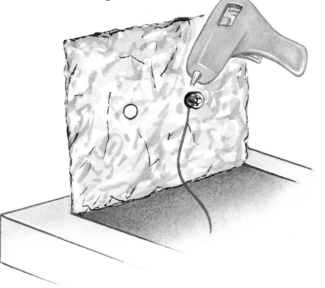

9 Cut two pieces of single-strand wire 10 cm (4 in.) long and remove 2.5 cm (1 in.) of insulation from each end. Wrap one end of each wire into a small circle. Glue a circle to the metal connector at the bottom tip of each lightbulb. Twist the bare ends of these two wires together. Use the scissors to make a hole in the back of the box, near the edge, and poke this twisted connection inside the box.

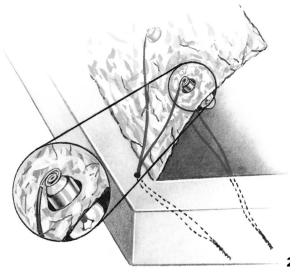

29

10 Cover one side of each piece of cardboard with aluminum foil, shiny side out.

11 Cut a 2 m (6$^{1}/_{2}$ ft.) piece of double strand wire and remove 2.5 cm (1 in.) of insulation from each end of both strands.

12 Tape one bare strand of wire to the aluminum foil side of each piece of cardboard. Be sure to use the two bare strands from the same section of wire.

13 Cut four 5 cm (2 in.) strips from the sock or fabric. Tape the strips to the aluminum foil as shown. This will keep the two pieces of foil from touching each other until someone steps onto the cardboard and squeezes them together.

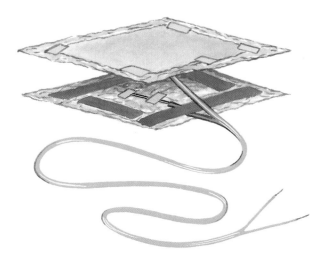

14 Put the two pieces of cardboard together with the foil sides facing each other and tape around the edges.

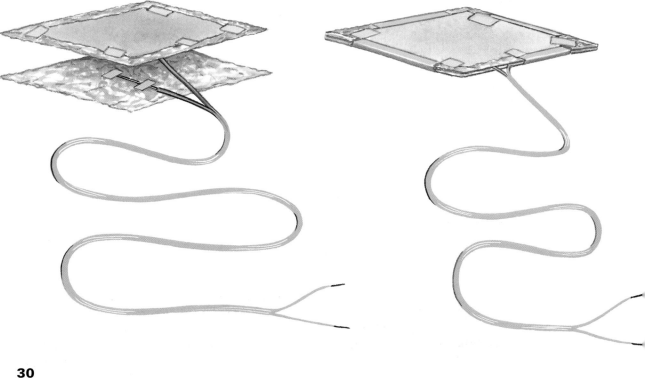

15 Connect the wires as shown and tape your box shut. Try out your new sign by stepping on the pad and watching the light come on. If the light stays on, you may need to add more fabric between the cardboard.

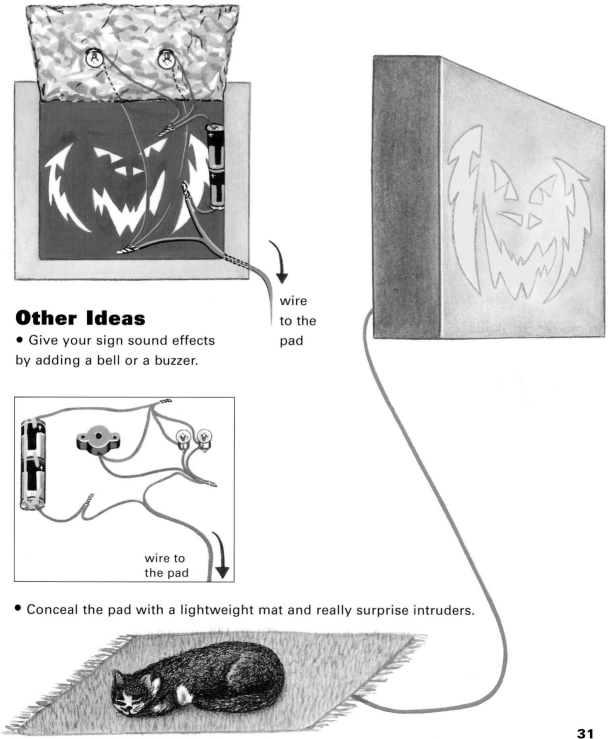

wire
to the
pad

Other Ideas

• Give your sign sound effects by adding a bell or a buzzer.

wire to
the pad

• Conceal the pad with a lightweight mat and really surprise intruders.

Super Car

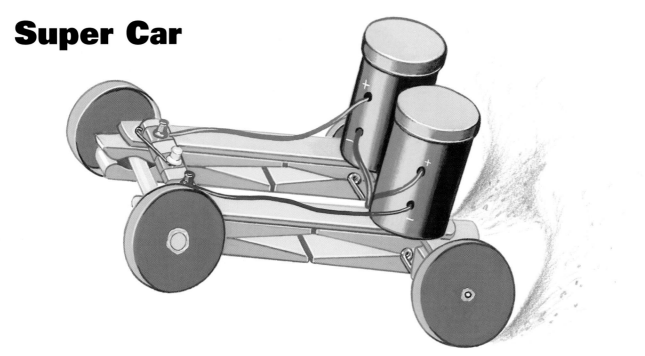

You will need

2 battery packs (see page 9)

4 clothespins

4 Popsicle sticks

glue

2 DC motors (1.5 V)

a hacksaw

dowel about 13 cm x 0.5 cm
($5^1/_2$ in. x $^1/_4$ in.)

a nail

4 lids from plastic film
containers

plastic electrical tape

scissors

3 push pins
(red, blue and yellow)

wire (24 gauge, single strand)

1 Glue a clothespin to each end of a Popsicle stick. Repeat with a second stick. These are the car's main frame sections.

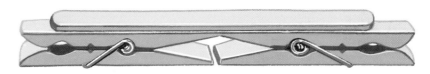

2 Glue a motor to each end of another Popsicle stick so that the motor shafts are facing out. This is the motor section.

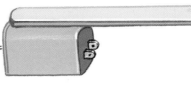

3 Clamp the motor section into one end of each frame section as shown. This will be the back of your car.

4 Cut a piece of dowel and the last Popsicle stick about 4 cm (1½ in.) shorter than the motor section. Slip the dowel into the holes of the clothespins at the other end of the car frame. If the dowel cannot turn freely, slip a small piece of Popsicle stick in the clamping end of each clothespin.

5 Use the nail to punch a hole in the center of each film-container lid. Slide a lid onto each end of the dowel and each motor shaft, for wheels. Secure each wheel with some glue.

6 Wrap some tape around the short Popsicle stick. Push a red push pin into one end of the Popsicle stick, a blue pin into the other end, and a yellow pin into the center. Glue this assembly to the car frame, behind the front wheels.

7 Glue a battery pack above each motor.

8 Twist together the bare end of wire from the top hole of one battery pack with the bare wire from the bottom hole of the second battery pack.

9 Cut four pieces of wire 15 cm (6 in.) long and remove 2.5 cm (1 in.) of insulation from each end.

10 Connect one piece of wire tightly to each connector tab on the motors. Secure the connections with a drop of glue.

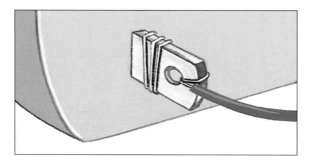

11 Twist together the bare end of wire from one motor connector with a bare end of wire from the second motor. Then twist this pair of wires together with the pair of twisted wires from step 8.

12 Twist the remaining ends of bare wire from each motor together and around the yellow push pin, as shown.

13 Wrap the remaining end of bare wire from one battery pack around the red push pin and the other around the blue push pin, as shown.

14 Cut a piece of wire 6 cm (2 1/4 in.) long and remove all the insulation. Wrap one end around the yellow pin. Make a hook with the other end.

15 Test your car by touching the bare wire from the yellow pin to the red pin — the wheels should go in one direction. Next, touch the bare wire to the blue pin — the wheels should go in the opposite direction.

16 If the wheels do not reverse direction, try reversing one of the batteries in your packs.

17 If the motors don't spin in the same direction, reverse the wire connection on one motor.

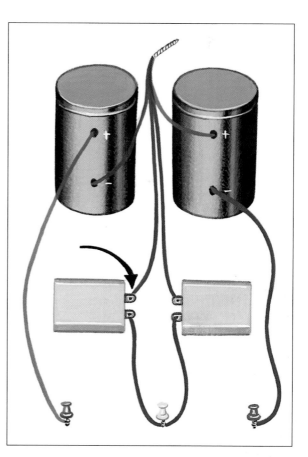

Rumble Box

You will need

2 battery pads (see page 8)

a pencil and scissors

masking tape

a nail

small box
(no smaller than
10 cm [4 in.] square)

wire
(24 gauge, single strand)

glue

straws (0.5 cm [1/4 in.]
diameter works best)

cardboard

aluminum foil

small long-nose pliers

a DC motor (1.5 V)

a C cell battery (1.5 V)

a small elastic band

an eraser

gift wrap and bow

1 Stick a piece of tape on the center of each side of the box. Use a nail to punch four small holes about 1 cm (1/2 in.) apart through the tape on each side.

2 Cut nine 25 cm (10 in.) pieces of wire and remove 5 cm (2 in.) of insulation from each end.

3 Thread a bare end of one piece of wire from inside the box out through one hole and in through the hole beside it. Continue threading it out and in until you've secured the entire end. Tape over the bare wire on the inside of the box. Repeat with seven more wires in the other pairs of holes.

4 Make a frame on one side of the box, as shown, by gluing on four pieces of straws, cut to size. Frame the other three sides the same way. The straws will keep the pressure switch open until someone picks up the box and squeezes the switch.

5 Cut out four pieces of cardboard the same size as the sides of your box. Cover them on both sides with aluminum foil.

6 Tape the squares over the straws. These sides form the switches. Be careful not to tape too tightly or the switches will stay closed, activating the motor before you're ready.

7 Tightly twist together one bare wire from each side of the box. Then twist together the remaining four bare ends, as shown.

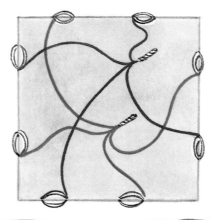

8 Use pliers to tightly twist the bare end of wire from a battery pad together with one group of four wires.

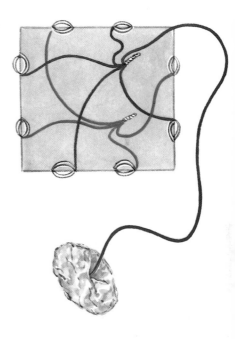

9 Connect the bare end of wire from the second battery pad to one of the connector tabs on the motor.

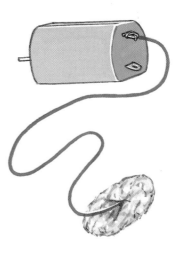

10 Trim 2.5 cm (1 in.) of bare wire from the last piece of wire from step 2. Connect this wire to the remaining tab on the motor and the remaining group of four wires. Secure each connection with a drop of glue.

11 Place a battery between the two pads and stretch an elastic around them to keep them together. Test your work by holding the box on opposite sides and squeezing. Release and then squeeze the other sides. With each squeeze the motor should start running. Cover each connection with tape.

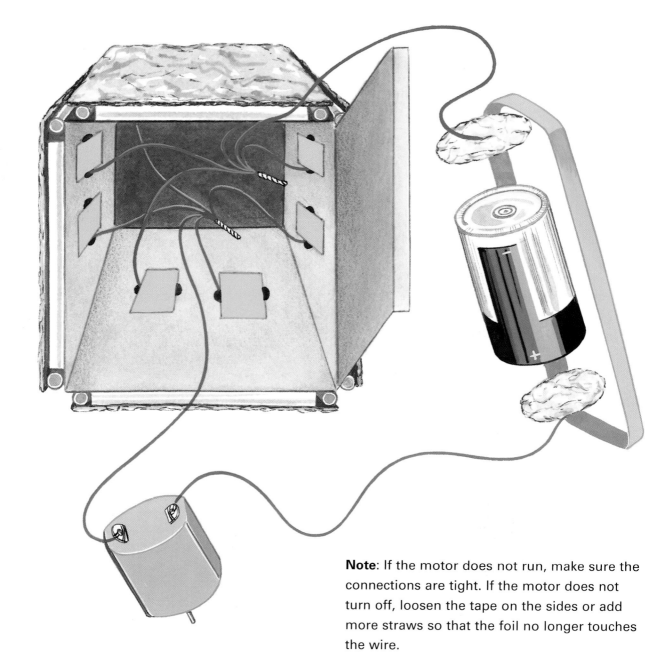

Note: If the motor does not run, make sure the connections are tight. If the motor does not turn off, loosen the tape on the sides or add more straws so that the foil no longer touches the wire.

12 Cut a piece of eraser about 2.5 cm x 2.5 cm x 0.5 cm (1 in. x 1 in. x $^1/_4$ in.) Using a sharp pencil, punch a small hole in a corner of the eraser. Push the motor shaft into the hole. The eraser should spin off-center. This is what creates the rumbling.

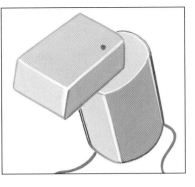

13 Glue the battery to the bottom of the box, and then glue the motor to the battery. Be sure to leave enough room for the eraser to spin freely.

14 Test the box again. When everything works well, wrap up the box to look like a gift and wait for someone to pick it up.

Other Ideas

• Use a bell or buzzer instead of the motor. Be sure to connect the buzzer positive to positive.

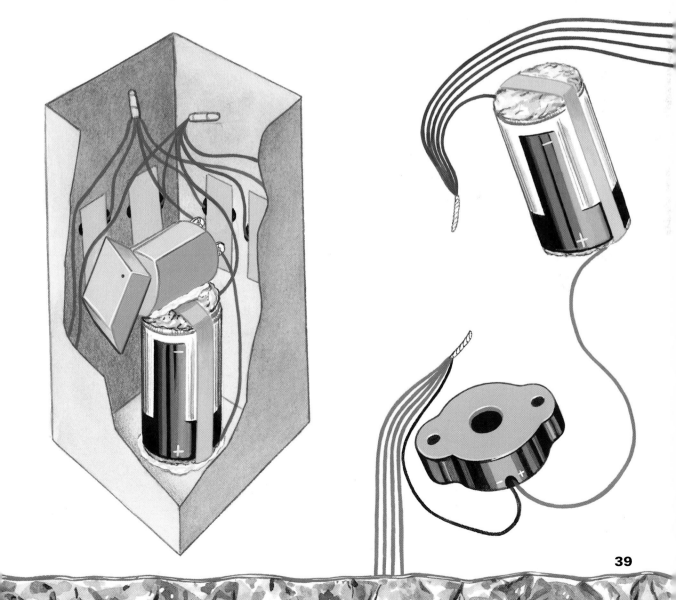

Wiper Glasses

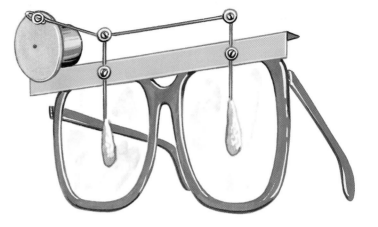

You will need

a 15 cm (6 in.) piece of 2 cm x 0.25 cm ($^3/_4$ in. x $^1/_8$ in.) L-shaped aluminum

a hacksaw

an old pair of sunglasses or safety glasses with plastic frames

a marker and ruler

a drill with a 0.25 cm ($^1/_8$ in.) drill bit

wire cutters

1 m (3 ft.) of 14 gauge copper wire

a finishing nail

a hammer

a hot-glue gun

cotton balls

8 flat washers, 0.25 cm ($^1/_8$ in.)

5 metal screws 0.25 cm x 1 cm ($^1/_8$ in. x $^1/_2$ in.)

a screwdriver

a pair of pliers

10 hex nuts, 0.25 cm ($^1/_8$ in.)

plywood (2.5 cm x 2.5 cm x 0.5 cm)

a compass

a DC motor (3 V)

a battery (6 V)

wire (24 gauge, single strand)

1 L round plastic bottle

3 clothespins

aluminum foil

The frame

1 Use the hacksaw to cut the aluminum 4 cm (1$^1/_2$ in.) longer than the glasses. This frame should fit snugly over the glasses and extend beyond them at one end.

2 Find the center of each lens and mark it directly above onto the frame of the glasses and the aluminum frame. Try to line up the marks on both frames.

3 Drill holes in the spots marked on both of the frames. Place the aluminum frame over the glasses frame and check that the holes still line up.

The wipers

4 Cut two pieces of copper wire 9 cm (3$\frac{1}{2}$ in.) long. Remove all the insulation from both pieces.

5 Bend each piece of wire around the finishing nail to create a small ring with a hole in the center, about the same size as the metal screws. You'll use these rings to attach the wipers to the frame and glasses.

6 If necessary, hammer the ring area of each wire until it is flat.

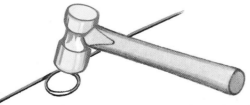

7 Bend another ring the same size in one end of each piece of wire. You will use these rings to connect the wipers to the link rod (see step 9) and the motor. If necessary hammer these rings until they are flat.

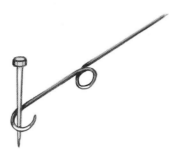

8 Glue pieces of cotton balls to your wipers so they'll really wipe.

The link rod

9 Measure the distance between the two holes in the aluminum frame. Cut a piece of copper wire long enough to bend a small ring in each end and still reach between the holes. This piece links both wipers together once they are connected to the frame.

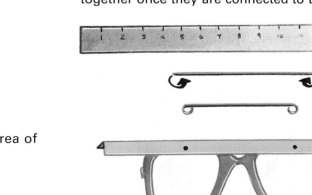

Assembling the pieces

10 Place a washer onto a screw and slip the screw through the center ring of one of the wiper blades, followed by a second washer. Pass the screw through the hole in the aluminum frame and the hole in the glasses frame. Thread two nuts onto the end of the screw. Repeat for the second wiper blade.

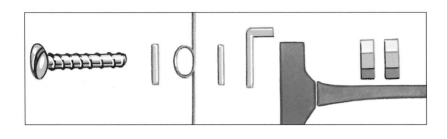

11 Connect the link rod to the top hole in each wiper blade using the method shown in step 10.

The fly wheel

12 Find the center of the plywood square by drawing a diagonal line from each corner. Use a compass to draw a 2.5 cm (1 in.) circle inside the square. Cut off the corners with the hacksaw.

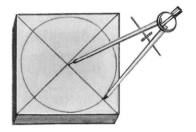

13 In the center of the circle drill a hole that is slightly smaller than the shaft on the motor. This circle will drive the wiper blades, so it must be tight or it will not spin when the motor is on.

14 Drill a 0.25 cm ($1/8$ in.) hole in the outer edge of the circle, as shown. This is where the drive rod (see step 17) will be connected.

Mounting and connecting the motor

15 Secure the fly wheel to the motor shaft so that it will not slip when the motor is running. Use some glue to be sure it will stay on.

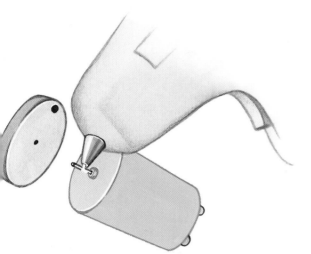

16 Glue the motor with its fly wheel onto the end of the aluminum frame so that the center of the fly wheel aligns with the link rod.

The drive rod

17 Turn the fly wheel so the hole is at the bottom and position the wiper blades straight down. Cut a piece of copper wire about 2 cm (1 in.) longer than the distance from the hole in the fly wheel to the top ring of the closest wiper blade, with the blades in this position. Bend one end of the wire into a small ring, the other into an oval.

18 Follow the diagram to ensure you have everything lined up correctly. Use a screw to connect the oval in the drive rod to the fly wheel. Thread two nuts onto the end of the screw. Connect the other ring to the link rod.

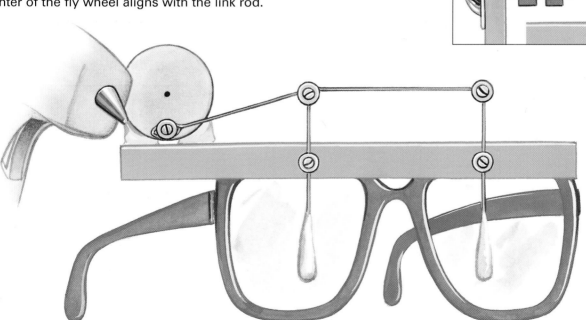

Note: The glasses will work best if all the mechanical joints are a little loose.

Testing the wiper action

19 Once everything is mounted and connected, slowly turn the fly wheel by hand to feel for any tight spots. A tight spot is usually caused by a misaligned joint or an over- or undersized length of rod. Try bending the rods a bit until things move smoothly. If you still have trouble, make a new link rod or drive rod that fits better.

Connecting the wires

20 Make a 6 V battery holder and wire clamps similar to those you made for the Squirt Finger (see steps 6 to 9, page 25). Use single-strand wire for the connections, as shown.

21 Connect the battery to the motor using a push-button switch (see page 10). Glue the switch to the battery holder. Try out your glasses by closing the switch and watching the wipers move. If you want your glasses to run more slowly, use a smaller battery.

More Gadgets and Gizmos

Tilt on/off light

By using an empty plastic bottle and a
metal washer, you'll be able to make a
switch that opens and closes just by
turning it over the way this light works.

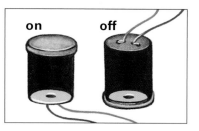

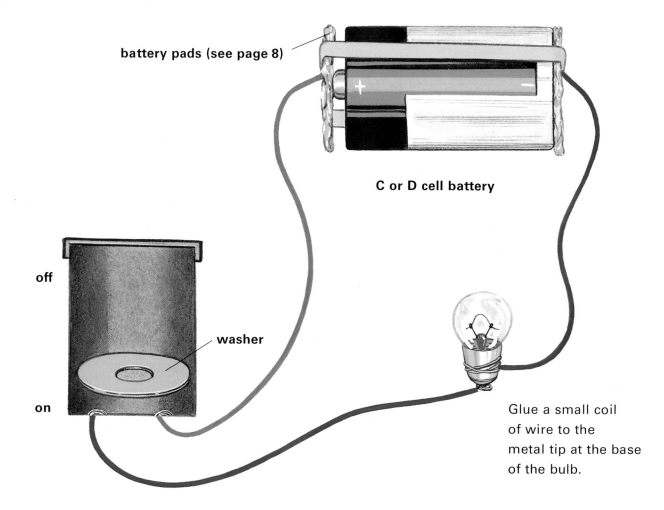

battery pads (see page 8)

C or D cell battery

off

washer

on

Glue a small coil
of wire to the
metal tip at the base
of the bulb.

Poke two holes in the bottom of the
bottle. Insert a small section of wire
through each hole. Secure each wire
with glue on the outside of the bottle.

Three-speed fan

Give any gadget more than one speed by arranging the batteries following these fan instructions.

small DC motor (1.5 V)

battery packs (see page 9)

Attach a propeller to the motor shaft.

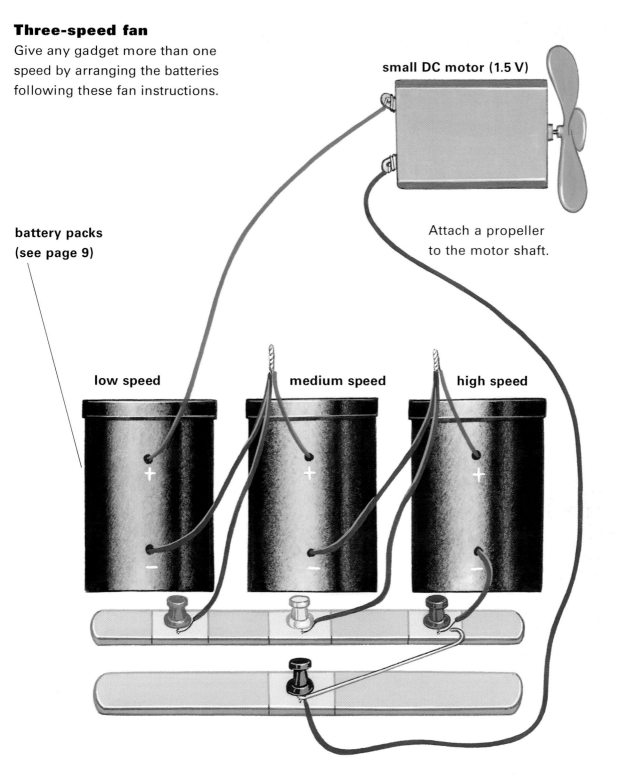

low speed medium speed high speed

Make a triple hook switch (see page 11). Touch the hook to the first push pin for low speed, the second push pin for medium speed and the third for high speed.

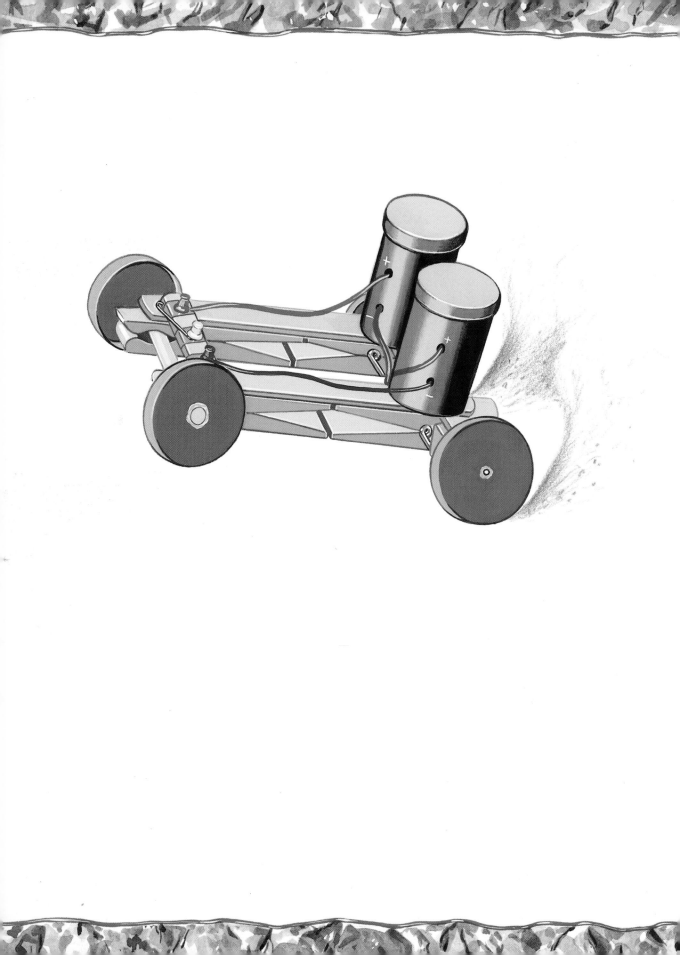